COLOR NOTE MONSTERS

a nifty notespeller to write and play
by SHARON KAPLAN

This delightful book helps develop many skills. Students identify the notes and intervals as they color the pictures, and they write missing notes in the Monster music. That step involves an understanding of note location on the staff, rhythm values, and stem directions. Titles help the students think about how the piece should sound, and the dynamics necessary for that sound.

This workbook/performance book reinforces note-reading and interpretation skills, and is a lot of fun! Enjoy!

Editor: Carole Flatau

CONTENTS

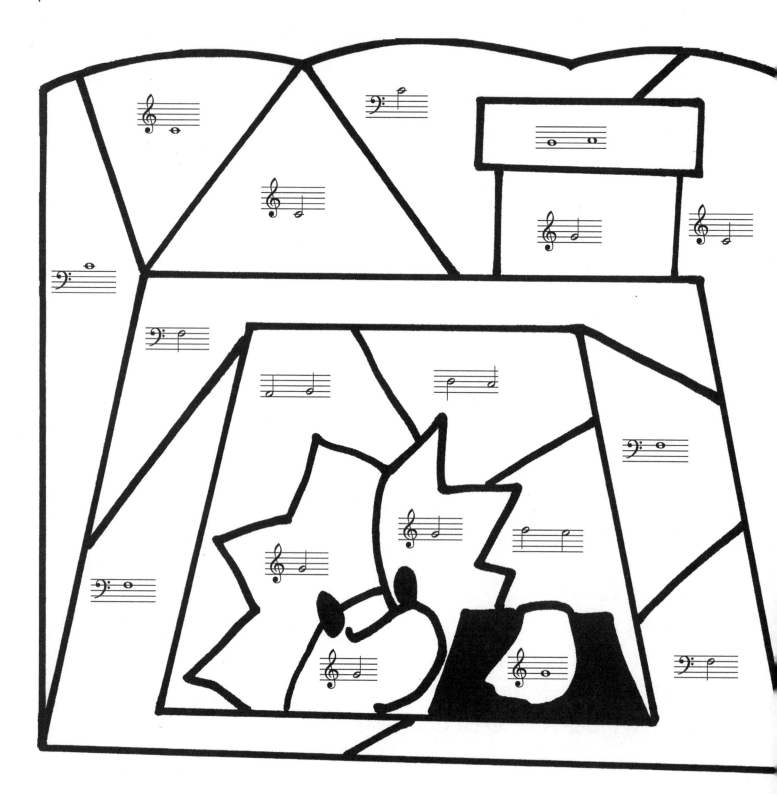

COLOR   C - blue

F - black

G - red

2nds - gray

MONSTER HIDES IN THE ATTIC

Write in the missing notes. The letter names tell you which note to use. If the letter is above the staff, add a RH note. If the letter is below the staff, add a LH note.

Be sure that you use the correct time value for the note so that when you add up the notes and rests you will have 4 counts for each hand.

Add dynamics (p and f) where you think they should be.

Play this Monster piece.

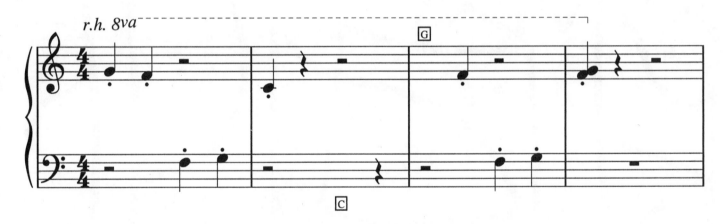

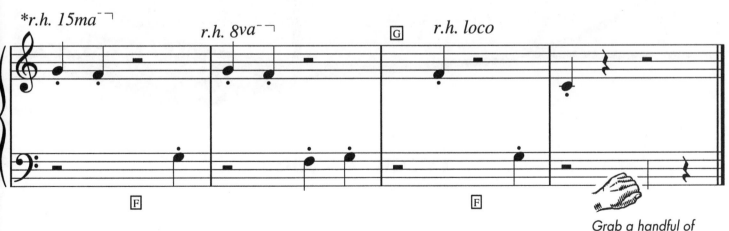

Grab a handful of
notes at the bottom
of the keyboard.

*15ma above notes means play them 2 octaves higher.

6

COLOR **C - yellow**

G - brown

F - blue

2nds - orange

3rds - green

MONSTER IN THE MANOR

Add the missing notes using the correct time values. Remember that the value of the notes in each measure must add up to 3.

Add *legato slurs* over each 4 measure phrase.

Add your own dynamic marks.

Play.

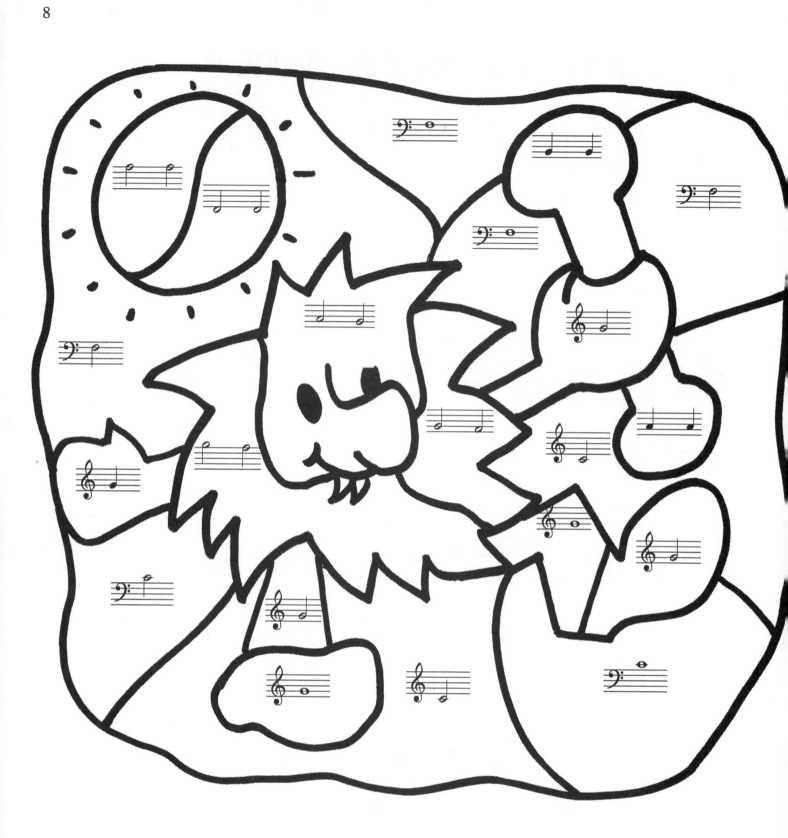

COLOR C - green

F - blue

G - purple

2nds - pink

repeated notes - yellow

MONSTER MARCHES

Add the missing notes using the correct time values. Remember that the value of the notes in each measure must add up to 4.

Add your own dynamic marks.

Play.

(LH crosses over RH)

MONSTER HAS A LITTLE LAMB

Add the missing notes using the correct time values. Remember that the value of the notes in each measure must add up to 4.

The song needs words. Can you write some?

Add slurs to show where Monster breathes.

Add *tempo indication* and dynamic marks.
(The tempo indication tells how fast or slow to play.)

Play the piece.

> The Monster picture for this piece is on page 12. It is after the piece so you don't have to turn pages while you play.

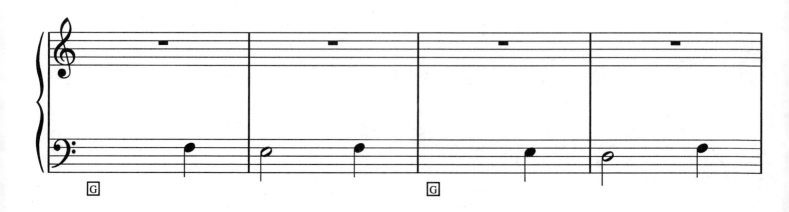

12

COLOR **E - blue**

F - light purple

G - pale pink

3rds - yellow

4ths - green

13

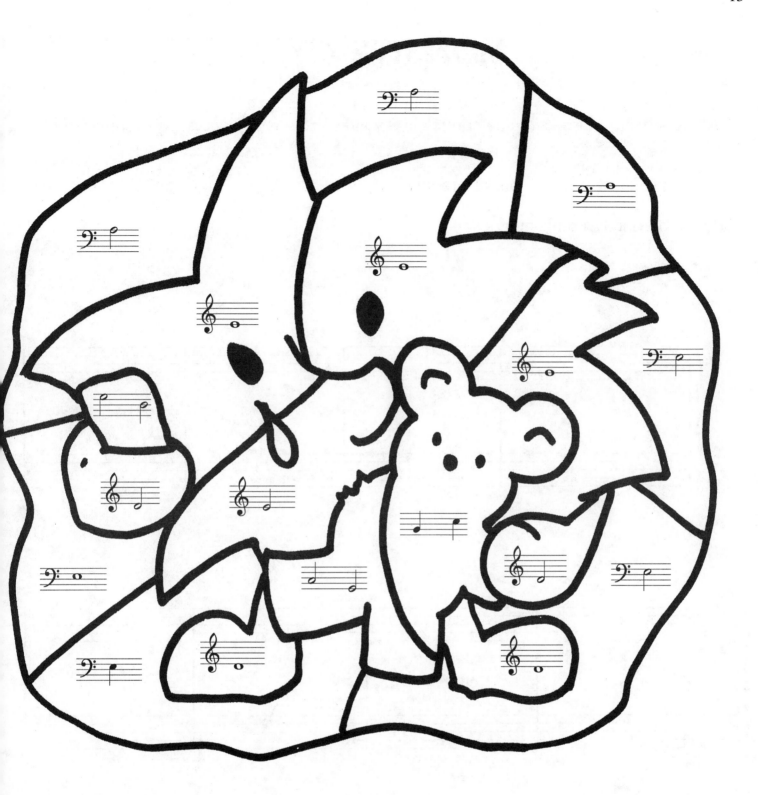

COLOR   A - pink

𝄞 **D - light purple**

𝄞 **E - light blue**

𝄢 **E - violet-red**

4ths - light brown

MONSTER CRIES

Add the missing notes using the correct time values. How many beats will there be in each measure?

Add slurs to show where Monster breathes.

Add tempo and dynamic marks.

Play the piece.

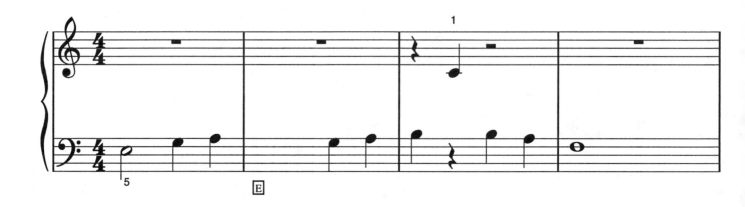

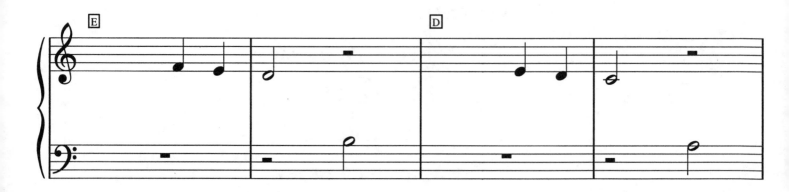

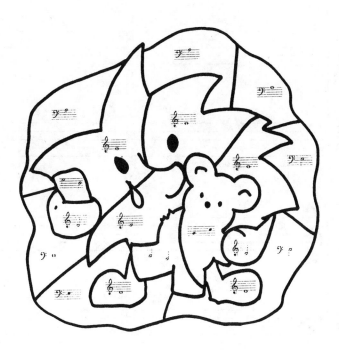

MONSTER DANCES

Add the missing notes.

Add *staccato dots* where you think the monster is hopping in the dance.

Add your own dynamic marks.

Play the piece.

This Monster's picture is on page 18.

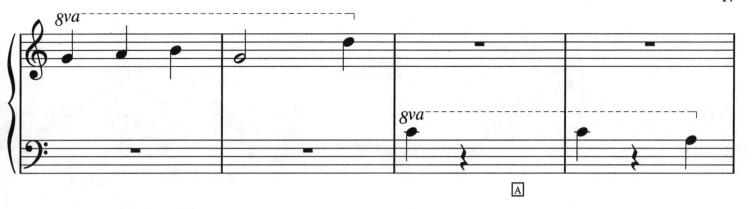

A

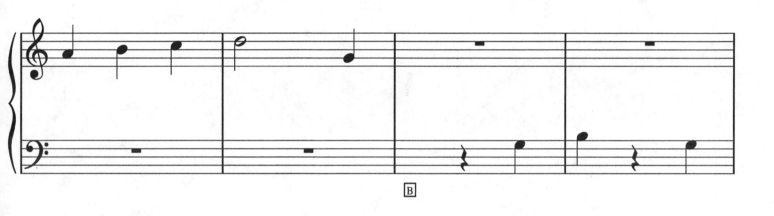

B

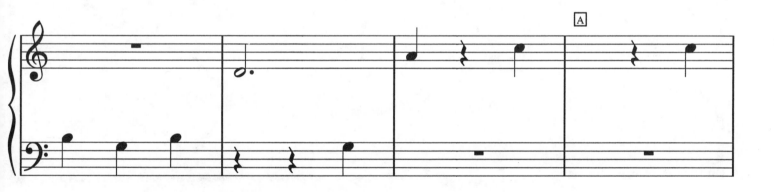

A

8va

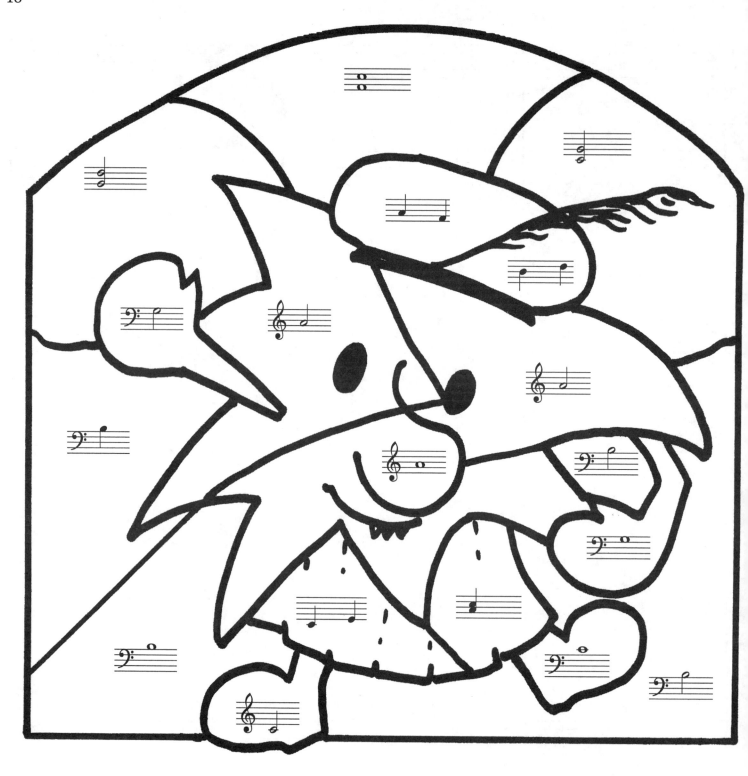

COLOR   A - red

B - light green

C - orange

G - yellow

3rds - dark green

5ths - blue

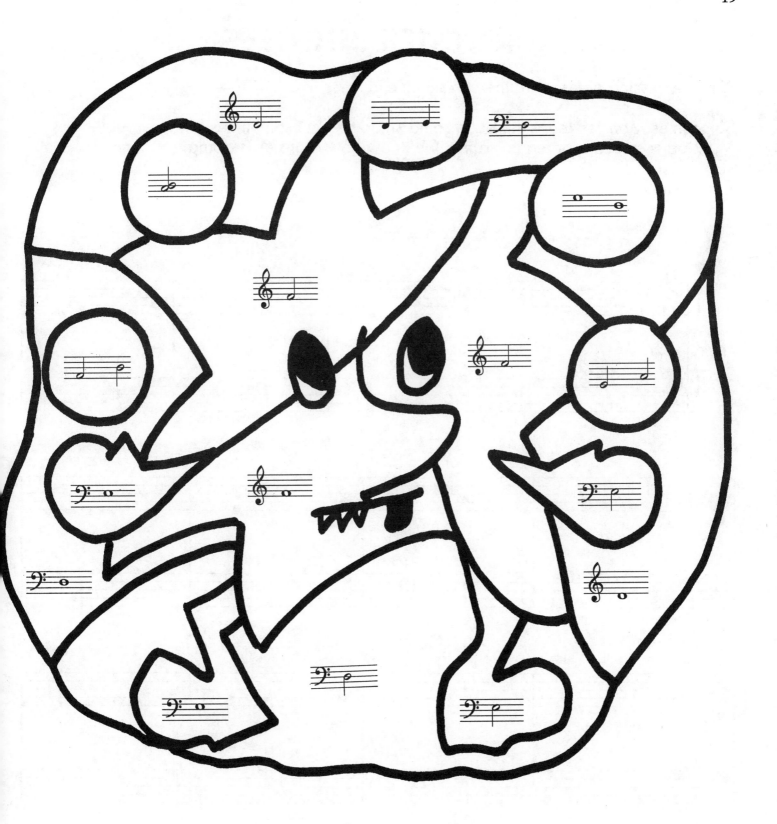

COLOR   D - yellow

E - blue

F - orange

2nds - red

4ths - purple

MONSTER JUGGLES

Add the missing notes using the correct time values.

Sometimes Monster keeps the balls going smoothly, but sometimes he has trouble.
Mark parts staccato or legato so that we know how Monster is doing.

Add your own dynamic marks.

Play the piece.

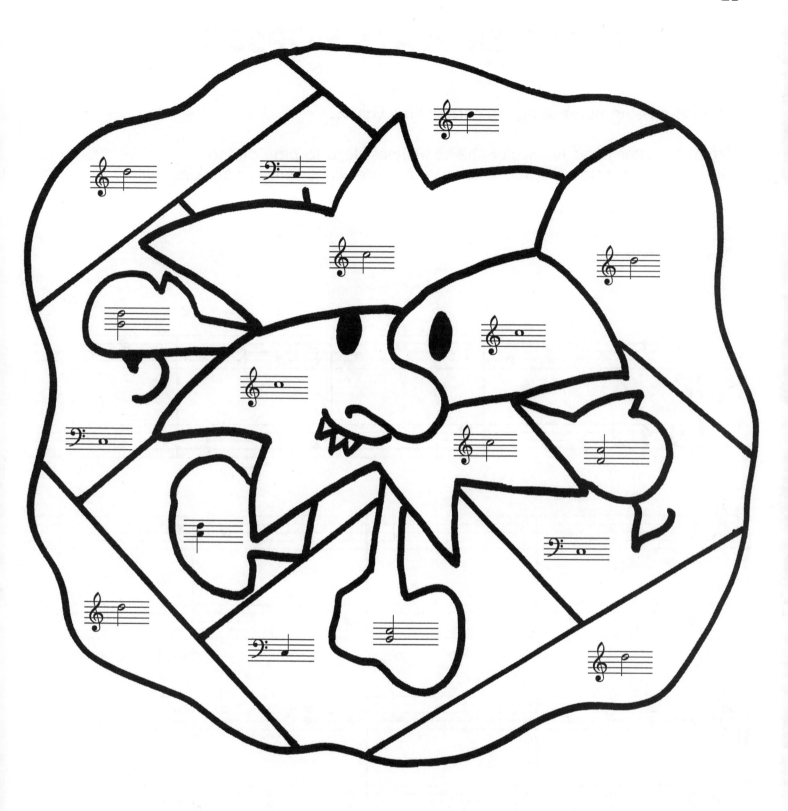

COLOR 𝄞 **C - pink**

𝄢 **C - light brown**

D - violet

4ths - black

5ths - light blue

MONSTER PLAYS HOPSCOTCH

Add the missing notes using the correct time values.

When Monster plays hopscotch, he sometimes stops to plan ahead.
Mark parts staccato or legato to tell us if Monster is hopping or thinking.

Add your own dynamic marks.

Play the piece.

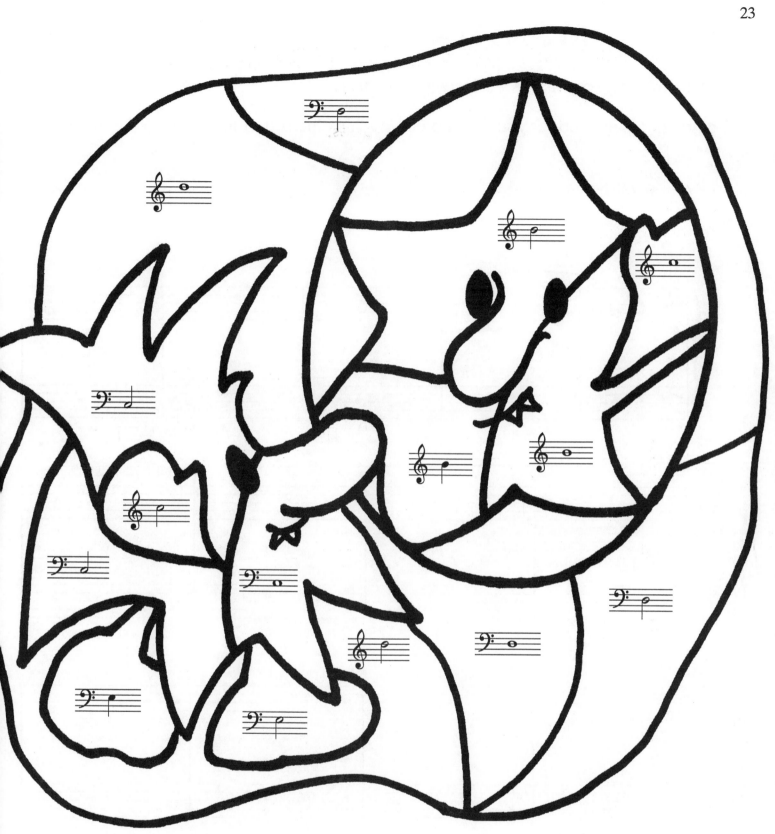

COLOR   B - pink

𝄞 **C - blue**

𝄢 **C - red**

D - yellow

E - brown

MONSTER IN THE MIRROR

Add the missing notes using the correct time values.

The first slur is marked for you. Where do you think the rest of them go? Write them in the music.

Add your own dynamic marks.

Play the piece.

25

COLOR A - orange

B - yellow

C - gray

D - blue

E - red

F - black

G - green

MONSTER RIDES A BUMPER CAR

Add the missing notes using the correct time values.

Where is Monster bumping into other cars or the wall? What marks can you put on the music to tell us?

Play the piece.